CHASING THE STORM

TORNADOES, METEOROLOGY, AND WEATHER WATCHING

RON MILLER

TWENTY-FIRST CENTURY BOOKS / MINNEAPOLIS

This book is dedicated to
Yazmin and Jemima Forde.

Twenty-First Century Books
A division of Lerner Publishing Group, Inc.
241 First Avenue North
Minneapolis, MN 55401 U.S.A.

For reading levels and more information, look up this title at www.lernerbooks.com.

Library of Congress Cataloging-in-Publication Data

Miller, Ron, 1947– author.
  Chasing the storm : tornadoes, meteorology, and weather watching / by Ron Miller.
    pages   cm
  Includes bibliographical references and index.
  ISBN 978–1–4677–1284–2 (lib. bdg. : alk. paper)
  ISBN 978–1–4677–2546–0 (eBook)
  1. Tornadoes—Juvenile literature. 2. Storm chasers—Juvenile literature. I. Title.
QC955.2.M55 2014
551.55'3—dc23   2013009291

Manufactured in the United States of America
1 – DP – 12/31/13

TABLE of CONTENTS

CHAPTER ONE
A DAY IN THE LIFE OF A
STORM CHASER

YOU ARE A STORM CHASER. YOU START YOUR DAY BEFORE DAWN. IT IS STILL DARK outside when you are at your computer, checking weather data on the Internet. You have a long list of sites to check. One of these is the Storm Prediction Center, operated by the National Oceanic and Atmospheric Administration (NOAA). Located in Oklahoma, the job of the Storm Prediction Center is to forecast severe thunderstorms and tornadoes. Its website features maps and other data that detail any severe weather occurring in the United States.

You see that there are signs of a severe storm. It is several hundred miles away from where you are. But there is a strong possibility that it might generate tornadoes. You grab a quick breakfast and head for the car. You have a lot of driving ahead of you. A friend who shares your interest in storms is going to join you, and she says to stop by her house to pick her up. This is good news since it's a smart idea to have someone along to share the driving and to act as an extra observer. You and your friend will also share the navigating, using a GPS (Global Positioning System) device to keep track of exactly where you are in relation to the storm. This will also allow you to take the shortest and quickest routes. A storm can disappear as quickly as it formed, so time is of the essence.

Storm chaser George Kourounis measures wind speed in Florida just hours before Hurricane Dennis made landfall in July 2005. Dennis was the first major hurricane of the season that year, followed the next month by Hurricane Katrina, the costliest natural disaster in the United States.

Along the way, your friend periodically checks for weather updates on her tablet. Things look good. The storm is still brewing. While you focus on the road, your friend keeps an eye on the sky. She is looking for telltale signs of a big storm. For example, she's keeping an eye out for the huge, towering clouds that indicate the formation of a supercell. Supercells are where tornadoes are born.

You are lucky today. You spot a tornado!

IN THE EYE OF THE STORM

Real-life storm chasers have dramatic stories to tell. For example, storm chaser George Kourounis remembers chasing Hurricane Katrina in the Gulf Coast of the United States in 2005. He remembers that "during Hurricane Katrina, the wind was blowing so hard that I had to crawl across the ground or risk getting blown away completely! There were pieces of metal flying around, spinning in the air like the blades of a helicopter, and every drop of rain felt like a needle stabbing me in the face. It was a very scary day for me, but luckily I was with a team of other experienced storm chasers and we were all looking out for each other."

"My most exciting adventure," says professional storm chaser Roger Hill, "was probably in South Dakota on June 24, 2003, when we witnessed sixteen tornadoes in a single day. The final tornado had wind speeds of more than 200 miles [320 kilometers] per hour. It wiped the small town of Manchester, South Dakota, off the face of the earth. Best part is nobody was killed. We had relayed reports to the local authorities of the tornado, who relayed them to the National Weather Service to issue warnings. Folks took it serious, fortunately."

The excitement can sometimes be a little too close to home, as storm chaser David Reimer discovered. "My most exciting adventure," he says, "occurred on April 3, 2012, in Dallas, Texas. We were expecting severe weather, but weak wind shear [the turbulence when winds at different levels and speeds meet] was expected to keep any risk of tornadoes low. It turns out that an outflow boundary, or a rush of air out of a thunderstorm, had pushed into the area from storms the previous night. The result was an increase in wind shear across the Dallas-Fort Worth area. When I started the chase that morning, I didn't expect to see a tornado. By the time all was said and done, I ended up watching a large tornado move through areas I had called home."

The tornado damaged or destroyed dozens of homes, tossed big trucks through the air as if they were toys, and left tens of thousands of people without power. "Even to this day," Reimer says, "I still have anxiety when I think about what happened."

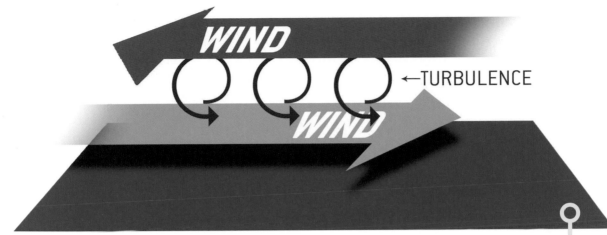

Wind shear is the turbulence created by a difference in wind speed and direction over a relatively short distance in Earth's atmosphere.

One of the most exciting adventures for professional storm chaser Caryn Hill was her first solo chase. "I recognized the signs of a tornado," she recalls, "and knew what they meant. I was able to safely chase it. I was one of only three chasers out there. I think that was the first time the other chasers took note that I could do it on my own!"

WHY CHASE STORMS?

People have been chasing tornadoes and other violent storms for a very long time. They do this for many reasons. Many storm chasers are scientists. Scientists and researchers hope to learn how tornadoes form and how they work. Data, photos, and videos gathered by storm chasers have enabled scientists to create detailed computer models of tornadoes. These models have helped forecasters make more accurate predictions about the formation and behavior of the storms. This in turn has saved countless lives and prevented billions of dollars in damages. Some scientists even hope to eventually control or prevent tornadoes and other storms.

Other people chase storms for a living. They hope to obtain exciting photos and video of tornadoes. They earn money by selling these images to television stations, newspapers, and magazines—while at the same time adding to the general knowledge of tornadoes. Storm chasing is also a recreational activity, and several companies offer storm-chasing tours. "I think there's a little storm chaser in all of us," says professional storm chaser Roger Hill. "I became interested in tornadoes and storms," Hill continues, "when I was a child. At nine years old, the house I was living in was hit with a powerful tornado. . . . From then on I was fascinated by storms and tornadoes and in 1985 started chasing them on my own."

Kourounis explains his career this way: "When I was growing up, I always had an interest in science and nature, and as I got older those interests grew to include travel, adventure, photography, and exploration. Chasing storms has allowed me to combine all those things that I love into a career and lifestyle that has taken me all over the world." He says of his career, "I didn't start chasing

Robin Tanamachi is a research meteorologist and a storm chaser. She participated in VORTEX2, a major two-year project in the Plains region of the United States. The purpose of the project was to study the structure and formation of tornadoes to improve weather forecasting. Here, she stands next to her Doppler radar truck in Nebraska.

THE COST OF TORNADOES

On May 20, 2013, the small town of Moore, Oklahoma, was hit by one of the largest tornadoes on record. Like many such storms, the Moore tornado was part of a much larger weather system that gave birth to numerous other tornadoes. The giant 1.3-mile-wide (2.1 km) storm was classified as an EF5 tornado, the most powerful known tornado. The tornado lasted thirty-nine minutes and traveled 17 miles (27 km). During that time, winds of 210 miles (338 km) an hour killed 24 people and injured 377 others. Nearly half the fatalities were children who were in school at the time the tornado struck. The homes of 12,000 to 13,000 families were damaged or destroyed. Costs of this destruction may exceed $1 billion.

The tornado that struck Moore, Oklahoma (above), in May 2013 caused catastrophic damage to homes and to two elementary schools, neither of which had storm shelters. Of the twenty-four storm-related deaths, ten were children.

storms until I was in my twenties. Living in Toronto [Ontario, Canada] helped inspire my interest in storms because the CN observation and communications tower in downtown Toronto gets struck by lightning between 70 to 100 times per year! I still enjoy going downtown during a storm to watch the tower get struck."

Chasing tornadoes may seem like a crazy thing to do. But professional storm chasers are not daredevils. Howard Bluestein, who teaches at the University of Oklahoma, agrees. "We [storm chasers] believe we understand the structure of storms, and we do not put ourselves in any danger of being hit by a tornado."

While Bluestein and other professional storm chasers take every precaution, following storms is a very dangerous occupation. This was tragically proven true on May 31, 2013, when three storm chasers—Tim Samaras, Paul Samaras, and Carl Young—were killed by a powerful tornado in Oklahoma. The three men were experienced scientists with more than twenty years of tracking tornadoes. However, they were caught by a tornado that suddenly and unexpectedly changed direction. They were the first professional storm chasers to die while pursuing a tornado.

Kourounis knows his work is dangerous. He says,

"I just love photographing all aspects of nature, especially nature at its most extreme. Sometimes that means chasing tornadoes in Kansas or Oklahoma, sometimes it's trying to get into the eye of a hurricane in Florida, or sometimes I even find myself climbing to the summit of erupting volcanoes. These adventures all have elements of risk and excitement, but I try to do dangerous things in as safe a manner as possible.My scariest adventure was the Joplin, Missouri, tornado in 2011. We were racing down Ridge Line Road trying to get out of the way of the violent [EF5 tornado] as it barreled through town. At one point we had chunks of debris falling on the vehicles, and we had to hurry, warning people to take cover along the way. We missed getting hit by it by only three city blocks!"

Storm chaser Tim Samaras (*at the wheel*) monitors a storm from his chase vehicle with Carl Young (*at the computer*) and Jon Davies (*far left*). Samaras was a longtime storm chaser and an esteemed scientist and tornado expert. He died with his son Paul and storm-chasing partner Young during a violent tornado near El Reno, Oklahoma, in May 2013.

HURRICANE HUNTERS

Chasing a tornado in a car or a truck can be scary. But it is a special kind of well-trained storm chaser who will fly an airplane into the heart of a hurricane. A hurricane is a powerful storm more properly called a tropical cyclone. The word *tropical* means that these storms form over warm ocean waters. *Cyclone* comes from a Greek word meaning "whirling." It describes the circular motion the storms make.

Hurricanes are tropical cyclones that form in the Atlantic Ocean. In the Pacific Ocean, they are called typhoons. Although hurricanes form over open water, they can quickly move over land. Hurricanes are the largest, most powerful storms on Earth. Hurricane Sandy, which hit the eastern coast of the United States in October 2012, was 1,100 miles (1,770 km) wide. The wind in Sandy reached speeds of 115 miles (185 km) per hour, but winds in even larger hurricanes can reach speeds of more than 155 miles (250 km) per hour. In just two days, Sandy caused more than $75 billion in damage and killed as many as 285 people.

Since 1946 the US Air Force has operated a special unit that flies into the heart of hurricanes. These members of the Air Force Reserve 53rd Weather Reconnaissance Squadron are called the Hurricane Hunters. Typically, Hurricane Hunters fly large aircraft packed with scientific instruments deep into a powerful storm, sometimes flying as low as 500 feet (150 m) above the sea. Doing this is extremely dangerous. Five aircraft and their crews have been lost in the years since the program started.

The National Oceanic and Atmospheric Administration also operates its own unit of Hurricane Hunters, who fly aircraft equipped with scientific laboratories into the giant storms. Because hurricanes can create tremendous damage and loss of life, the information gathered by US Air Force and NOAA Hurricane Hunters is valuable. Knowing the speed of the winds, how fast the storm is traveling, and in what direction can save hundreds of homes and countless lives.

TOOLS OF THE CHASE

Storm chasers provide valuable information for weather scientists who are trying to learn how Earth's weather works. Whether chasing storms for science or business, most storm chasers travel with tablets and laptop computers, cameras, and instruments for measuring wind speed, temperature, and air pressure.

Most of these instruments are simple and can even be found around many homes. For instance, storm chasers measure temperature with an outdoor thermometer. They measure air pressure with a barometer. Most hardware and variety stores carry these. The instrument storm chasers use to measure wind speed is a little more unusual. Called an anemometer (from Greek words meaning "wind" and "measure"), it looks a little like a windmill. The faster the wind makes it spin, the higher the speed it registers.

Many storm chasers, says Kourounis, also "use instrumented vehicles or mobile Doppler radar trucks to gather scientific data about these storms, which helps us to learn more and more every year about how they form and develop. It is still a very young field of science, and there is still much to learn."

Scientists launch a meteorological balloon to gather storm information. The balloon carries instruments that measure temperature, pressure, and air velocity.

Storm chasers also release balloons near the path of a tornado. These balloons are like the ones you might see at a birthday party, except much larger. A typical weather balloon might be anywhere from 3 to 15 feet (1 to 3 m) wide. This is big enough to carry the various instruments, which are attached to a small radio that sends information back to the observer. Weather balloons are a key aid for storm chasers because they can provide information from much closer to a tornado than scientists can safely go.

DOPPLER RADAR

In recent years, Doppler radar has become one of the most important storm-chasing tools. It allows chasers to make extremely accurate measurements of a tornado's wind speed and direction of movement. The development of portable Doppler radar devices has enabled researchers to get such measurements from very close to a storm. Doppler radar instruments can be carried by cars or trucks.

The basic idea behind Doppler radar is simple. If you have ever heard a fire engine rushing along a road, you may have noticed how the siren seems to rise

CHRISTIAN DOPPLER

Christian Doppler was an Austrian scientist. Born in Salzburg in 1803, his name is attached to Doppler radar, one of the most powerful tools of modern meteorology. Doppler's discovery originally had nothing to do with weather. It came from his interest in astronomy. He wanted to explain why the color of a star seemed to be affected by whether it was traveling toward Earth or away from it. While his theory—now called the Doppler effect—originally dealt with light, it can be applied to anything that travels in waves. This includes radio and sound. By measuring the Doppler effect of the waves emitted or reflected by an object, a scientist can determine the speed at which it is traveling and whether it is moving toward her or away from her.

Doppler also did very important work in physics, astronomy, and mathematics. Never in very good health, he became ill from the strain of his work and died in Italy in 1853 at the age of forty-nine.

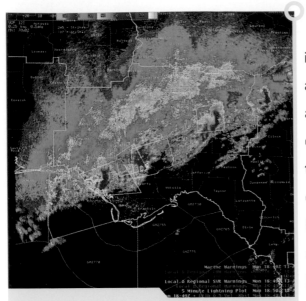

This Doppler radar image from the Tallahassee, Florida, area shows several bow echoes (bow-shaped patterns), which indicate strong winds capable of forming tornadoes. Areas in red indicate tornado warnings while those in yellow indicate severe thunderstorm warnings.

in pitch as it approaches you and lowers in pitch as it goes away. This is called the Doppler effect after Christian Doppler, the Austrian scientist who first described it in 1842. When a radar beam is bounced off a moving object, the same thing happens. If the object is moving away, the returning signal is lower in pitch. If the object is moving toward you, the returning signal is higher in pitch. Because the scientist knows exactly what the signal would be like if the object were standing still, she can precisely measure the speed at which the object is moving.

Not only does Doppler radar measure how fast a storm such as a tornado is moving, but it can also tell scientists how fast it is rotating. This is because one side of the storm is moving toward the observer as it rotates and the other side is moving away from the observer.

CHAPTER TWO
WHAT MAKES A
TORNADO?

A GOOD STORM CHASER KNOWS A LOT ABOUT TORNADOES AND OTHER STORMS. And understanding tornadoes is all about getting your mind around how the atmosphere of Earth works, what it is made of, and how it gets energy from the sun. You can think of the atmosphere as an ocean more than 60 miles (100 km) deep. All humans on Earth, including you, live at the bottom of this ocean. But instead of water, this ocean is made of gas. About 70 percent of this gas is a colorless, odorless gas called nitrogen. The rest is oxygen and a small amount of other gases such as carbon dioxide (CO_2).

Oxygen is that part of the atmosphere you need to breathe in order to stay alive. Oxygen gets thinner with altitude. Above 60 miles (100 km), there is so little oxygen that scientists consider this altitude to be the point at which outer space starts.

A column of air 1 inch (6.5 centimeters) square reaching from the surface of Earth to a height of about 60 miles (100 km) weighs 15 pounds (6.8 kilograms). So 15 pounds of air presses on every square inch of your body. This atmospheric pressure lessens with altitude because as you rise, there is less air pressing down from above. Think about how your ears pop as you rise in an elevator to the top of a very tall building. That's the effect of changing air pressure on your body.

THE EARTH'S ATMOSPHERE

THERMOSPHERE

Aurora

MESOSPHERE   80 km/50 miles

STRATOSPHERE   45 km/28 miles

Earth's weather takes place below this level.

ozone layer

TROPOSPHERE   Mount Everest   13 km/8 miles

All of Earth's weather takes place in the troposphere, the very lowest level of Earth's atmosphere. Weather is shaped by many factors, including the spin of Earth, wind patterns, and the heat of the sun, among other things.

The lowest part of Earth's atmosphere, from ground level to about 8 miles (13 km), is called the troposphere. All of Earth's weather—including tornadoes and other storms—takes place within the troposphere. Extending above the troposphere to about 30 miles (48 km) is the stratosphere. Most of the oxygen in the stratosphere is in the form of ozone. The oxygen we breathe is in the form of a molecule with two atoms (O_2). Ozone, on the other hand, has three atoms (O_3). Ozone is very good at filtering dangerous ultraviolet radiation from sunlight. Without the ozone layer, life on Earth would be impossible. Above the stratosphere is the mesosphere, which rises to about 50 miles (80 km). The uppermost layer is the thermosphere, which eventually merges with outer space.

WATER VAPOR EXPERIMENT

You will need the following:

> ice cubes
> a drinking glass
> water

Put some ice cubes in a glass and fill it with water. As the outside of the glass gets cold, droplets of water will form on the sides. This is water that was in the atmosphere. The cold glass caused it to condense into large droplets that you can see. The amount of water vapor in the air is called humidity. The higher the humidity, the more water vapor is in the air.

WEATHER

The sun is the ultimate source of power that drives Earth's weather. The sun warms Earth's surface and the oceans, and it evaporates water from rivers, lakes, and seas. As the sun warms lakes, oceans, and rivers, the water in them evaporates and rises into the atmosphere. On a clear day, this water vapor is invisible. We are aware of its presence only when it forms clouds or falls as rain or snow. Earth's winds help to distribute water vapor from areas with a great deal of water, such as forests and grasslands, to areas with little water.

Earth's tropical regions—the areas to the north and south of the equator—are warmer than the planet's poles because the sun shines more directly on the tropics. Because of this uneven heating, Earth's atmosphere swirls, with warm air rising and cool air rushing in to fill the space. Earth's rotation enters the picture too. At the equator, the planet spins at 1,000 miles (1,600 km) per hour, with the speed diminishing toward the poles. This rotation causes the currents of air to swerve to one side. For this reason, winds tend to move in spirals instead of straight lines. Sometimes these spirals, powered by warm ocean waters or warm land surfaces, tighten into whirling circular storms called hurricanes (water-based storms) and tornadoes (land-based storms).

THE CORIOLIS EFFECT

The effect of the spinning Earth on moving air currents is called the Coriolis effect. This effect causes air currents traveling between the poles and the equator to move in curves. A playground carousel shows how this happens. Think of two children riding the carousel on opposite sides. While the carousel is standing still, one tosses a ball to her friend. He will have no trouble catching it since it travels straight toward him. When the carousel is spinning, she tosses the ball to her friend again. Instead of traveling directly toward him, the ball curves away to one side. In exactly the same way, the Coriolis effect causes the winds on Earth to curve to one side or the other as they move between the equator and the poles. It is the Coriolis effect that makes storms such as hurricanes and tornadoes spin in circles.

THE CORIOLIS EFFECT

Air would move in straight paths if Earth did not rotate.

Rotation of Earth causes winds to take curved paths.

Rotation of Earth

The rotation of Earth causes winds—and wind-based storms—to move in circular patterns. This Coriolis effect also impacts the flow of ocean waters and the development of various types of ocean waves.

WEATHER PATTERNS

As large air currents pass over continents, oceans, mountains, plains, and deserts, these land features play a part in creating patterns of weather. For example, when warm, moist air runs into a mountain, it is forced to rise. This cools the air, which makes the moisture condense into clouds, rain, or snow. Once the air has passed over the mountain, it becomes much drier on the other side. For this reason, the side of a mountain range opposite the prevailing direction of air movement has less rainfall. In the United States, the land west of the Rocky Mountains has a great deal of rainfall. The eastern side has dry deserts.

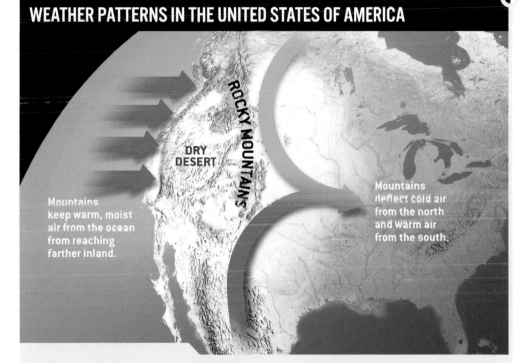

WEATHER PATTERNS IN THE UNITED STATES OF AMERICA

ROCKY MOUNTAINS

DRY DESERT

Mountains keep warm, moist air from the ocean from reaching farther inland.

Mountains deflect cold air from the north and warm air from the south.

This map of North America shows the ways in which major mountain systems such as the Rockies impact weather patterns across the continent.

THE BIRTH OF A TORNADO

A tornado begins with a thunderstorm—and not just any thunderstorm but an especially powerful one. Beneath the thunderstorm, fast winds high above the ground encounter slower winds near the ground. Imagine rolling a ball of clay on a tabletop with the flat of your hand. The clay will become a snakelike cylinder, rotating as your hand rolls it along. The same thing happens to the air between the thunderstorm and the ground. The fast-moving layer of wind beneath the storm causes the air beneath it to become a horizontal rotating cylinder just like the clay does under your hand. This effect is called wind shear.

The rotating tube of air then encounters powerful updrafts beneath the storm. These updrafts are caused by warm, moist air flowing upward from the ground. The updrafts pull on the rotating tube until it is vertical. The rotation of the tube then combines with the force of the updraft. The result is a whirling column of great strength called a mesocyclone (*meso* means "middle"). A mesocyclone is midway in size between a tornado and a full-size cyclone such as a hurricane. Storm chaser Roger Hill says, "I find the structure of a storm the most interesting. Sometimes when they are rotating, they look like a spaceship or a barber pole spiraling into the atmosphere at 60,000 feet [18,288 m]."

HOW A TORNADO IS FORMED

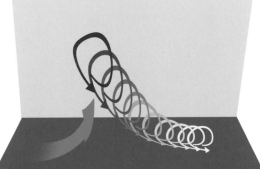

1. Wind shear creates a cylinder of rotating air.

2. An updraft lifts one end of the cylinder.

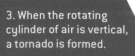

3. When the rotating cylinder of air is vertical, a tornado is formed.

Mesocyclones can be enormous, ranging from 2 to 50 miles (3.2 to 80 km) in diameter. They are also immensely powerful. And they give birth to tornadoes.

TORNADO SEASON

Tornadoes are most likely to occur in certain regions of the United States and at certain times of the year. In the Southwest and along a line stretching across the northern part of the country from the Dakotas through Connecticut, tornadoes are most likely during July, August, and September. In the Midwest, from Kentucky through Texas, tornadoes tend to cluster in April, May, and June.

In the Southeast, from Louisiana through Georgia and Florida, residents know to expect tornadoes during January, February, and March. Tornadoes occur so frequently in Arkansas, Iowa, Kansas, Louisiana, Minnesota, Nebraska, North Dakota, Ohio, Oklahoma, South Dakota, and Texas that this region is often called Tornado Alley.

Tornado Alley is an informal name for the region of the United States where 90 percent of the nation's tornadoes occur. In this region, cold, dry air from Canada and the Rocky Mountains meets warm, moist air from the Gulf of Mexico and hot, dry air from the Sonoran Desert. The resulting turbulence leads to powerful storm systems.

FROM DUST DEVILS TO CYCLONES

There are many kinds of tornadoes. The familiar summertime dust devil, seen in parking lots and empty fields, is a mini-tornado. Dust devils are usually harmless. They are not attached to a cloud, and they are rarely more than 3 feet (10 m) wide and a few hundred feet high. They typically last only a few minutes. Like its bigger, more dangerous cousin the tornado, a dust devil is a rapidly rotating column of air. This column forms as warm air rises rapidly over a large, flat, open surface that has been heated by the sun. Trees, buildings, and other structures tend to interfere with the formation of the rising column. This is why dust devils are seen so often over parking lots, large fields, deserts, and other areas with few obstructions.

Landspouts are weak tornadoes, while gustnadoes are whirlwinds created by sudden, intense bursts of wind on the gust front (the leading edge of cool air rushing down and out) of a thunderstorm. Downbursts are often mistaken for tornadoes. They are caused by columns of air suddenly sinking toward the ground. When they hit the ground, the air spreads out in powerful winds that can create a great deal of damage.

Tornado-like features form over water too. When they do, they are called waterspouts. Like dust devils, waterspouts rarely develop the power of tornadoes over land. They are also not associated with thunderstorms. Waterspouts, however, can become extremely large and can pose a danger to ships and aircraft.

Full-fledged tornadoes are the most dangerous. They are caused by air flowing rapidly up into a thunderstorm. Tornadoes can rate up to EF5 on the Enhanced Fujita (EF) Scale, making them among the most powerful storms on Earth. The Enhanced Fujita Scale is a meteorological system for classifying the strength and destructive force of tornadoes.

It rates the strength of tornadoes from EF0 to EF5. The scale was developed in 1971 by Tetsuya Fujita, a professor of climatology (the scientific study of Earth's climate) at the University of Chicago in Illinois. Originally called the Fujita Scale,

Dust devils such as this one form over broad, open areas with few obstructions. Unlike tornadoes, which form during thunderstorms, dust devils occur in warm, sunny conditions.

ENHANCED FUJITA TORNADO SCALE

EF5	>200 mph (>322 km/h)	incredible damage
EF4	166–200 mph (267–322 km/h)	devastating damage
EF3	136–165 mph (218–266 km/h)	severe damage
EF2	111–135 mph (178–217 km/h)	significant damage
EF1	86–110 mph (138–177 km/h)	moderate damage
EF0	65–85 mph (104–137 km/h)	gale: light damage

The Enhanced Fujita Scale ranks tornadoes by number (far left), wind speed (center), and extent of damage (right). In 2007 the Enhanced Fujita Scale replaced the earlier Fujita Scale, introduced in the early 1970s. The new scale better aligns wind speeds with associated storm damage.

it was revised in 2006 and officially adopted in 2007 to more accurately reflect the damage caused by high winds. The new scale is called the Enhanced Fujita Scale. Both dust devils and waterspouts usually rate no more than an EF0 on the Enhanced Fujita Scale.

CHAPTER THREE
WHAT'S GOING ON WITH THE WEATHER?

IN THE UNITED STATES, THE TORNADO SEASON OF 2013 GOT OFF TO A catastrophic start. Deadly tornadoes struck Oklahoma, killing twenty-four people in May and eighteen people, including three storm chasers, the next month. Many scientists believe these powerful storms are, in fact, coming more often and are getting worse. In the United States, for instance, the number of heavy rainstorms has doubled in the past fifty years. In that same time, the number of

A homeowner surveys damage to his property after a tornado hit El Reno, Oklahoma, in early June 2013. It was one of several tornadoes that devastated parts of Oklahoma that year.

tornadoes has been increasing by about fourteen per year. Experts suspect this trend may be linked to the fact that the average temperature of our planet has been slowly growing warmer. This pattern of global warming is a climate change and can affect the weather in many ways.

Weather and climate are often confused. Weather refers to changes in temperatures and precipitation from day to day or week to week. Climate, on the other hand, refers to the average temperatures and precipitation of a large area over a long period of time. To understand the distinction, think of a region with a dry climate, such as a desert. It can have rainy weather now and again. A place such as Hawaii, which has a rainy climate, can have sunny, dry weather. Overall, the climate of Earth has been gradually growing warmer as it slowly emerges from the last ice age, which ended only ten thousand years ago.

The warmer water gets, the faster it will evaporate. This is why clothes will dry faster in a clothes dryer or hanging out in the sun than they will if you hang them indoors. As Earth grows warmer, evaporation occurs at greater rates, bringing more water into the atmosphere from oceans and lakes. With more moisture in the atmosphere, the amounts of rain and snow in storms are greater. Storms that bring several feet of snow or even just a few inches of rain can cripple a city. They can slow or stop transportation, cause flooding, clog sewers, and bring down vital power lines.

In addition to creating more evaporation, more heat from the sun provides more energy for powering tornadoes and hurricanes. With more energy, storms are more violent and can last much longer. This increases the likelihood and scale of property damage and loss of human life.

GLOBAL WARMING

For many reasons, the average temperature of Earth has been gradually climbing over the past several centuries. One of the main reasons is the greenhouse effect. This phenomenon is related to the way Earth's atmosphere works.

The greenhouse effect is similar to an actual greenhouse, for which the effect is named. The glass panes of a greenhouse allow the infrared radiation of sunlight (which we feel as heat) to penetrate while preventing the heat inside from escaping. In the case of an airless planet, such as Mercury, the heat the planet's surface receives from the sun radiates back out into space. But if the planet has an atmosphere, like Earth does, the atmosphere acts like the glass roof of a greenhouse and traps much of the incoming solar radiation. Because the heat does not radiate back into space, the temperature at the planet's surface can become very high.

The carbon dioxide (and to some extent the water vapor) in Earth's atmosphere acts like the glass panes in a greenhouse. It allows the high-energy infrared radiation from the sun to pass through the atmosphere but prevents the low-energy infrared radiation from the surface from escaping back into space. The amount of carbon dioxide in our atmosphere is not yet so great that it keeps in

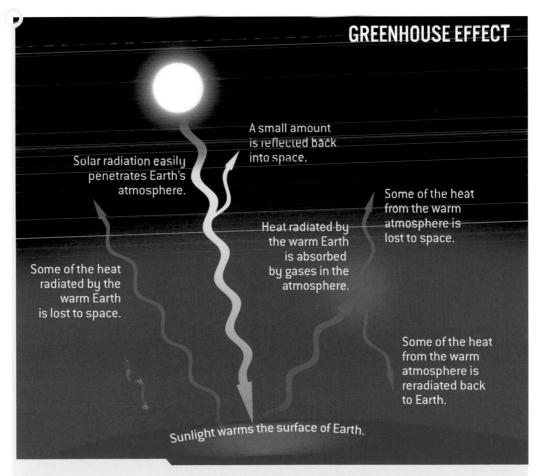

GREENHOUSE EFFECT

A small amount is reflected back into space.

Solar radiation easily penetrates Earth's atmosphere.

Some of the heat from the warm atmosphere is lost to space.

Heat radiated by the warm Earth is absorbed by gases in the atmosphere.

Some of the heat radiated by the warm Earth is lost to space.

Some of the heat from the warm atmosphere is reradiated back to Earth.

Sunlight warms the surface of Earth.

Earth's atmosphere naturally traps much (but not all) of the heat from the sun in a process known as the greenhouse effect. The more carbon dioxide in Earth's atmosphere, however, the more heat remains in the atmosphere.

GREENHOUSE EFFECT EXPERIMENT

You will need the following:

> a large glass jar (at least 1 quart, or 1 liter) with a lid
> dirt
> 2 thermometers

1. Turn the jar on its side, and put enough dirt in it to fill it level with the edge of the mouth of the jar.

2. Place the thermometer face up on the dirt, and put on the jar lid. Put the jar (still on its side) in a place where sunlight can shine directly on it.

3. Place the other thermometer alongside the jar. Wait for about an hour, and compare the temperatures.

You'll find that the thermometer inside the jar registers a much higher temperature. The reason is that the heat energy (infrared radiation) from the sun can pass easily through the glass, where it then warms up the dirt. The heat energy from the dirt, however, is not as strong as that from the sun so it cannot pass back through the glass. Instead, it is trapped inside the jar. Since more heat is coming into the jar than is being radiated away, the inside of the jar grows hotter than the outside air. In this experiment, the glass acts like the atmosphere of a planet such as Earth or Venus.

all the sun's heat. Most of the heat does manage to escape. However, the amount of carbon dioxide in Earth's atmosphere has been increasing dramatically. Today there is more carbon dioxide in Earth's atmosphere than there has been for the past four million years.

CARBON DIOXIDE ON THE RISE

Where is all this carbon dioxide coming from? Most of it is being created by people. It comes from the combustion of fossil fuels (petroleum, coal, and natural gas) in cars, factories, and power plants. Fossil fuels are the remains of ancient plants buried deep beneath the surface of Earth. Time (as in millions of years), temperature, and pressure change these plants into oil, coal, and natural gas. Because of their organic origin, fossil fuels are naturally rich in carbon. And when we burn these fuels, they combine with oxygen to create carbon dioxide.

Increasing levels of carbon dioxide in Earth's atmosphere are largely a result of the increase in the number of drivers and miles driven each year across the globe. Most meteorologists agree that human activity—such as reliance on carbon-based fuels—is behind the global warming with which high levels of carbon dioxide are associated.

Carbon dioxide is increasing in Earth's atmosphere for many reasons—and despite global efforts to reverse the trend. In the United States alone, for example, carbon dioxide emissions increased by about 10 percent between 1990 and 2011. In fact, in May 2013, NOAA announced that the amount of carbon dioxide in Earth's atmosphere was at its highest level in two million years. This is related to the nation's expanding population using more energy overall, by increased production of and reliance on the combustion of fossil fuels for electricity, and by drivers of cars and other motor vehicles putting on more miles each year. On a global scale, expanding economies in China, India, and many developing countries have led to the building of more factories, which rely on carbon-based fuels to power manufacturing. In addition, developing economies generally lead to a larger middle class, which has the money—and the desire—to purchase and drive cars. With more people around the globe driving more cars powered by fossil fuels, more carbon dioxide is released into Earth's atmosphere.

CAN WE CONTROL THE WEATHER?

Carbon dioxide and other emissions from cars and factories are having a real warming effect on the climate. Steve Rudin, a meteorologist for a television station, says, "I don't think we will ever be able to specifically control the weather, but I do believe mankind has had an impact on climate."

But can we control the weather to do what we want? Can we turn rain on and off? Can we stop a tornado or a hurricane? For more than half a century, a technique called cloud seeding has been used to create rain and to reduce the amount of fog and the size of hail. Originally developed in the United States, cloud seeding is used all over the world, especially in China, which has the largest cloud seeding program. The idea is based on the fact that rain drops form around tiny particles of dust. If an airplane flies over a cloud and "seeds" it by releasing small particles of a chemical (such as silver iodide) or dry ice (solid carbon dioxide), droplets of rain will form around the particles. Cloud seeding is common

The pilot of a cloud seeding plane steps over a row of flares containing silver iodide particles. When released into a cloud, the particles encourage the formation of rain. While some studies show no safety concerns related to the chemical, some environmental groups and researchers continue to investigate the chemical and its impact on soil, water, and mammal life.

at airports; at some ski resorts; and in some international cities such as Beijing, China, where governments want to bring more rain to dry areas.

Controlling or stopping a big storm is another matter. Storms such as hurricanes and tornadoes are very, very large and very, very powerful. Humans do not yet have the capability to control weather on such a grand scale. On a more limited scale, solutions to weather problems must take into account environmental and safety considerations. For example, when seeding clouds, care must be taken to use chemicals that do not endanger humans, animals, or plants. In another effort, to prevent water from evaporating into the atmosphere, Moshe Alamaro, a scientist working with the Massachusetts Institute of Technology, has suggested spreading oil over miles and miles of the surface of the ocean. Yet this might be as hazardous to sea life as an accidental oil spill.

Experts also worry that the ability to control weather might be used as a military weapon. For example, by causing a crippling drought or a devastating storm in an enemy country, a nation would create horrific human suffering and loss of life. From an ethical point of view, is controlling the weather worth it? Almost eighty nations—including the United States—have said no. They have signed on to an international treaty called the , which prohibits military use of environmental modification techniques. For now, researchers are still looking for ways to safely control weather patterns in ways that are both useful and safe.

CHAPTER FOUR
METEOROLOGY
ON THE JOB

PEOPLE WHO LOVE THE WEATHER AND WANT TO MAKE A LIVING AT IT HAVE various career opportunities. Andrew Snyder, for example, is a meteorologist with the National Weather Service (NWS). He explains why he became a meteorologist. "I've been interested in weather since my childhood. I can't pinpoint a time or certain weather event that sparked the interest, but I was always scared of thunderstorms when I was little. My dad was also very in tune with the weather for his job (forestry), so watching and hearing about the weather so much may have rubbed off on me."

The word *meteorology* might sound like the study of meteors, or shooting stars, but it's really the study of Earth's weather. Yet the two ideas—meteors and meteorology—are related. The words *meteors* and *meteorology* come from the same ancient Greek word *meteoron*, which means "a thing high up."

Meteorology is the study of Earth's weather, and meteorologists are the scientists who do the studying. It's a very old science. The Greek philosopher Aristotle wrote a book in 340 BCE called *Meteorologica*. It wasn't until the seventeenth and eighteenth centuries, however, that weather-tracking instruments such as the thermometer and barometer were invented. These tools enabled scientists to make accurate measurements and keep detailed records of changes in the weather. In addition, with the invention of the telegraph in the early nineteenth century, meteorologists from around the world could easily compare notes about how storms and other weather systems move. This was a very important scientific advance since conditions in one place can affect the weather 1,000 miles (1,600 km) away.

Before modern methods of communication, weather records were handwritten. An assistant for the Office of Coast Survey (now part of NOAA) took these notes to accompany his drawing (*bottom left*) of a waterspout observed over a small island off the coast of Florida in 1869.

MEET A METEOROLOGIST

Snyder loves the changes in weather. He says, "I personally enjoy the variability of meteorology. The weather can be very different from day to day and location to location. The challenge of figuring out what is going to happen and why it happens is what I find most interesting about meteorology."

HOW FAR AWAY IS THAT THUNDERSTORM?

Sound travels at about 1,126 feet (343 m) per second. Light travels 300 million times faster than that. This is why you see lightning before you hear the thunder it creates. The flash from the lightning gets to your eyes a lot faster than the sound gets to your ears. Sound takes about five seconds to travel 1 mile (1.6 km).

Knowing this, you can estimate how far away a thunderstorm is from where you are. All you need to do is count the number of seconds between a flash of lightning and the clap of thunder. Divide that number of seconds by five, and you'll know how far away the storm is in miles. To figure out the distance in kilometers, all you need to know is that sound travels 1 kilometer (0.6 miles) in about 2.9 seconds. So to figure out how far away a storm is in kilometers, divide the number of seconds by 2.9.

Snyder likes his job because "no two weather systems are the same or occur with any regularity. As a result, the job isn't monotonous and often poses challenges. Calm weather may allow for "routine" days, but that can change in an instant. It isn't a typical desk job; you are always active and involved. I enjoy the more hands-on approach to everyday forecasting. I find the fast pace more interesting and engaging, and there is always something new to learn."

WHAT DOES A METEOROLOGIST DO?

Meteorologists do many different things, depending on where they work and on which portion of the field their knowledge is concentrated. The different jobs can be classified into five main areas.

BROADCASTERS

The primary role of broadcast meteorologists is to deliver weather forecasts and information on television, radio, and the Internet. Broadcasters generally have additional duties at the station besides being an on-air voice. These duties include gathering information from sources such as NOAA and the National Weather Service, interviewing experts and other meteorologists, creating weather maps and other graphics, and visiting the scene during or after a weather disaster.

Lightning is a discharge of electricity. It occurs within a thunder cloud, between clouds, between a cloud and the ground, or from a cloud into the air. This lightning bolt strikes the ground in the southwestern United States.

FORECASTERS AND OPERATIONAL METEOROLOGISTS

The primary duty of forecasters and operational meteorologists is to observe current weather and to predict future weather. They do this continually as new information becomes available. Forecasts can be made over a variety of different time scales. Most people are interested in the daily forecast. Will it rain on our picnic? Should we close the windows tonight? Forecasts can also be made several days and even weeks in advance. These forecasts serve many different interests. Farmers need to know whether to expect rain or a dry period or if a damaging frost is on its way. The fishing industry needs to be aware of the possibility of storms at sea. Airlines need to know if bad weather will force them to change the route of a flight or even to cancel it. City officials need to know if a heavy snow is coming so they can prepare snowplows.

The federal government (such as the NWS) and privately owned forecasting companies hire weather forecasters. While the NWS serves the citizens of the United States as a whole, commercial weather companies usually appeal to a specific customer. Commercial weather companies offer a wide array of services, including weather apps and providing weather data to international governments. These companies may also sell meteorological equipment and/or software.

Meteorologist Monica Bozeman tracks a tropical storm at the National Hurricane Center in Miami, Florida.

Forecast positions may also be available with the aviation industry and other companies whose businesses have high stakes in weather forecasts. These jobs often involve rotating shift work as well as holiday and weekend work.

RESEARCHERS

Researchers work to discover new science, to improve existing science and knowledge, and to develop new methodologies to understand and predict weather. Researchers may take part in a specified mission or a job assignment such as developing more accurate computer models. They may join a collaboration of researchers on projects or receive grant money from a university or the government to conduct their own research. Researchers are employed by the government, universities, privately owned companies, and other research institutions. Researchers are most likely to work a predictable daytime work schedule, although demands and deadlines can lead to long hours.

CONSULTANTS

A relatively new sector of meteorology is in consulting work. A weather consultant's primary role is to interpret weather information for clients who need personalized and specific expert analysis. Such expertise includes testifying in a court case in which weather conditions are a key piece in determining the guilt or innocence of the accused. Consultants may guide the weather-impacted decisions of energy companies that build and maintain wind-powered generators. Consultants with experience may be self-employed, while others work for private weather companies or government agencies.

MILITARY METEOROLOGISTS

Weather is crucial to many military operations. Meteorologists and trained military service members are needed in many capacities, especially in observing and forecasting. Often a person in the military receives on-the-job training without first receiving a formal degree in science.

Forecasters with the NOAA Storm Prediction Center monitor weather conditions. One of the center's newer services is to alert the public to weather conditions that could lead to tornadoes during the night, when most people are sleeping. Warnings are available online and through NOAA weather radios.

EDUCATIONAL REQUIREMENTS

What kind of education do you need to become a meteorologist? At a minimum, meteorologists usually must have a bachelor's degree in meteorology/ atmospheric science. In the US military, however, a meteorology degree is not required because on-the-job training is offered. For some weather-related careers, a second degree in science, math, engineering, economics, or communication may be beneficial. For many research positions, a doctoral degree is required. If you think you might be interested in a weather career, you can start by taking classes in science, physics, and mathematics.

All meteorologists rely on computer models, so a familiarity with computer modeling is another important skill. Computers enable scientists to keep track of millions of pieces of information from all over the world. Computers also enable scientists to create models of weather. By feeding weather data into the computer, meteorologists can re-create weather systems, allowing them to better understand how weather works.

CHAPTER FIVE
OFFICIAL
WEATHER WATCHERS

MONITORING AND REPORTING WEATHER AND STORMS IS THE WORK OF MANY people and organizations. The organizations around the country that track weather patterns, issue forecasts and warnings, and monitor the climate rely on scientists. But they also count on observations from trained volunteers— including storm chasers and weather spotters—all over the United States.

THE NATIONAL OCEANIC AND ATMOSPHERIC ADMINISTRATION

Scientists working with the National Oceanic and Atmospheric Administration study the weather and climate affecting the United States. Through the National Weather Service, the NOAA issues daily weather forecasts and severe storm warnings. It also monitors the climate and its effect on the fishing industry and the nation's coastlines. NOAA was created in 1970 by combining several individual government science agencies, such as the United States Coast and Geodetic Survey, the Weather Bureau, and the Bureau of Commercial Fisheries.

NOAA maintains about fifteen hundred stations across the United States. The agency also maintains a large number of stations at sea. These are among the most important stations because 71 percent of Earth is covered by oceans and seas. If NOAA depended on its land-based stations alone, it would miss nearly three-quarters of the world's weather data. In addition to stations in the United States, NOAA also has access to the information gathered by many thousands of weather stations in other countries.

NATIONAL WEATHER SERVICE

The National Weather Service is an agency within the US government and is part of the NOAA. Its mission is to provide weather, water, and climate data, as well as forecasts and warnings, for the protection of life and property and enhancement of the national economy. NWS forecasts and warnings serve aviation, hydrological, marine, and general weather interests. NWS operates through a network of national and regional centers as well as 122 local offices. In addition to publishing national weather maps and forecasting rain and snow, it issues flood, tornado, and hurricane warnings. Through the Internet, much of the data and information generated by the National Weather Service is available freely to the general public.

The NWS works with state and city emergency management agencies as well as TV, radio, and Internet broadcasters to provide the public with an awareness of current weather events. It also works to prepare the public for potential hazardous weather situations.

NATIONAL WEATHER SERVICE COOPERATIVE OBSERVER PROGRAM (COOP)

Created in 1890, the COOP of the twenty-first century involves more than eleven thousand volunteers. The volunteers come from all walks of life: farmers, students, stay-at-home parents, fans of fishing and other outdoor activities, and many other people. They record weather observations on farms, in cities, at national parks, at seashores, at sea, and on mountaintops. The purpose is to gather weather data such as maximum and minimum daily temperatures and amounts of rain, snow, and other precipitation. This data is then relayed to the

TORNADO SAFETY

You and your family can stay safe during a tornado by following these National Weather Service guidelines:

• Listen to local radio and television stations or check online for weather updates.

• Watch for the signs of a tornado. These can include strong, persistent rotation in the cloud base; whirling dust or debris on the ground under a cloud base (tornadoes sometimes have no visible funnel!); and hail or heavy rain followed by either dead calm or a fast, intense wind shift. Many tornadoes are wrapped in heavy precipitation and can't be seen. A loud, continuous roar or rumble in the day or night that doesn't fade in a few seconds like thunder may be a sign.

• In a home or building, move to a predesignated shelter, such as a basement.

• If an underground shelter is not available, move to an interior room or hallway on the lowest floor and get under a sturdy piece of furniture.

• Stay away from windows.

• Get out of automobiles.

• Do not try to outrun a tornado in your car. Instead, leave it immediately and seek shelter.

• Mobile homes, even if tied down, offer little protection from tornadoes and should be abandoned.

• Occasionally, tornadoes develop so rapidly that advance warning is not possible. Remain alert for signs of an approaching tornado. Most deaths and injuries are caused by flying debris from tornadoes.

• After the tornado moves through your area, watch out for any fallen electrical power lines. Do not touch them! Check radio, television, or Internet updates after the storm for information or instructions specific to your area.

NWS and the NOAA to help scientists there to better understand the climate of the United States and how it may be changing over long periods of time. The data also helps meteorologists make more accurate forecasts and warnings about dangerous storms such as tornadoes and hurricanes.

Storm chaser George Kourounis agrees. "One thing that storm chasers are great for," he says, "is sending in our storm reports to the authorities. The meteorologists have no way of knowing for sure if a rotating storm is actually

Firefighters and volunteers are often the first on the scene after a tornado hits. In this photo, first responders and a citizen volunteer search for a dog after a tornado struck Adairsville, Georgia, in early 2013. The storm killed one person, flipped vehicles, and demolished buildings.

producing a tornado. Whenever we spot one, we let the National Weather Service know, so that they can issue a tornado warning for the next town in the path of the tornado. We'll never know how many lives we've saved over the years. Whenever we come across anybody who needs our help, whether it's after a tornado passes, or during a hurricane, we always stop to help out. There have been numerous times when we've stopped chasing to lend assistance to people in the disaster zone."

Cooperative observers allow the NWS to place weather-recording instruments such as rain gauges, thermometers, wind speed indicators, and barometers on their property. This can be any place in the open, such as a backyard or a field, or even a rooftop—as long as the location follows NWS standards. For instance, a rain gauge must be located in a place sheltered from the wind but not too close to trees and buildings. Weather-recording instruments measure daily changes in the weather, including the amount of rainfall or snowfall, wind speed and direction, and temperature. The observer must be willing to record these measurements and send them to the NWS.

Just about anyone can become a Cooperative observer. You can find out how to be a COOP volunteer by visiting the National Weather Service Cooperative Observer Program website at http://www.nws.noaa.gov/om/coop/become.htm.

SKYWARN

Skywarn is a volunteer program run by the NWS. It consists of nearly 290,000 trained severe weather spotters. Unlike a storm chaser, a weather spotter normally stays in one place and shares observations with the NWS by e-mail or phone when a severe weather event is pending or is in progress.

Skywarn volunteers help keep their local communities safe by providing accurate reports of severe weather. This information enables the NWS to issue more timely and accurate warnings for tornadoes, severe thunderstorms, and flash floods. The NWS has 122 local weather forecast offices (WFOs), each with a warning coordination meteorologist who is responsible for administering the Skywarn program in that local area. Training is conducted at these local offices and covers topics such as the basics of thunderstorm development, how to identify potential severe weather, what sort of information to report and how to report it, and basic severe weather safety.

Almost anyone can be a Skywarn weather spotter. To find out how to be a Skywarn volunteer, go to http://www.stormready.noaa.gov/contact.htm for more information about the program and to find a schedule of classes in your area and other local information.

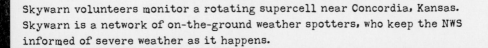

Skywarn volunteers monitor a rotating supercell near Concordia, Kansas. Skywarn is a network of on-the-ground weather spotters, who keep the NWS informed of severe weather as it happens.

CHAPTER SIX
BEING A
STORM CHASER

MANY PEOPLE WONDER IF THERE IS A ROLE FOR AMATEUR METEOROLOGISTS IN tracking and reporting the weather. "Yes!" says meteorologist Steve Rudin. "You can train to become a storm spotter and send snow measurements to local television stations or the local National Weather Service office. You can also join the American Meteorological Society (AMS) or the National Weather Association (NWA) as a student member."

"Storm chasers," Roger Hill adds, "relay information to local authorities so that warnings can be issued. Further, most storm chasers take tons of video and photographs, which they share with scientists and the NWS offices to use for research and training. Some storm chasers have weather instruments on their vehicles to record observations during the event [that] are shared with the science community."

"If you're going to be a storm chaser," David Reimer adds, "you have to be passionate about weather. There is a lot of driving, frustration, and exhaustion. Some people may not find that it is worth it in the end. That's how you separate the real storm chasers from those who just go out because of the movies and shows."

FOR THE LOVE OF WEATHER

The majority of storm chasers are amateurs. They chase storms as a hobby. Some storm chasers create clubs so they can share expenses and experiences. The Texas Storm Chasers group is typical of these organizations. It is, according to Reimer, "a small group of individuals that enjoy the complexities of severe weather. While we started out in 2009 just chasing storms, the evolution of social media has allowed us to spread our passion of weather. Today, we maintain a weather blog to inform the general public of upcoming weather hazards."

Very few people make a living at being a storm chaser. "The Discovery series *Storm Chasers*," says Reimer, "has made the impression that every time you go out chasing you get amazing storms and a hefty paycheck from a video. That couldn't be farther from the truth."

Only a handful of scientists, photographers, and tour operators make a living at storm chasing. Professional storm chasers such as George Kourounis sell photos and videos. Others, like Roger and Caryn Hill, give tours in addition to selling photos.

While the scientists usually have jobs at a college or a university or work for the government, amateur storm chasers sell video or photographs to pay their expenses. And storm chasing is a very expensive hobby. The biggest expense is usually gasoline. Following even a single storm system may entail traveling almost 1,000 miles (1,600 km) from Iowa to Texas in less than a week. And even after that trip, a chaser may never actually spot a tornado. In fact, many storm chasers feel lucky if they spot just one tornado for every ten times they go on a chase.

GOOD ADVICE

Kourounis offers some good tips for anyone who is thinking about becoming a storm chaser. "Anyone who is interested in storm chasing," he says, "needs to learn a lot about weather and how to make accurate forecast predictions. Sometimes I need to plan where I think a tornado might form up to two days in advance. That's tough to do, especially when these storms move quickly. Just jumping in your car whenever there's a tornado warning won't work. You'll either see nothing at all or put yourself in danger. I've spent a lot of time learning from other storm chasers, and their tips and tricks have really helped out over the years."

The hobby also requires patience. "Storm chasing," says Caryn Hill, "involves a trial and error type of learning curve, and those who think they will bag a tornado their first time out are being overly optimistic! Luck does have a lot to do with it!"

A group with a storm-chasing tour watches a severe storm in southern Nebraska.

Learning as much about weather, severe storms, and how they work is vital. "The more you know about meteorology," says Kourounis, "the better off you will be." Roger Hill agrees. "For someone who wants to be a storm chaser," he says, "I would recommend taking the National Weather Service spotter training. They offer a basic class and an advanced class. Any online education or courses from a university always help as well. Finally, I would recommend hooking up with someone who is an experienced storm chaser to ride along with to learn the ropes. Usually offering to split fuel costs is a great incentive to get someone to take you along." This is exactly what Reimer did. "I attended a severe weather training class," he says, "conducted by my local National Weather Service office. After completing my training, I started out chasing by simply driving up the road to watch our summertime thunderstorms, which were puny in comparison to Mother Nature's worst. By the time spring of 2009 arrived, I was chasing with an

Storm chaser Sean Casey moves his armored Tornado Intercept Vehicle (TIV) in a parking lot in Nebraska. Chasers rely on TIVs to shoot IMAX footage from within a tornado. Casey was part of VORTEX2, which studied tornadoes and supercell thunderstorms.

A young man tends to his backyard weather station. A home weather station is a great way to track and learn more about the weather in your area.

experienced friend who taught me much of what I know today."

Caryn Hill believes that it also takes "street smarts" to become a successful storm chaser. Someone wanting to chase storms, she says, "needs to have the will to learn how to read the weather models and then, more importantly, the storms."

The most important things to keep in mind are that storms are very dangerous and that chasing them is not as glamorous as it is portrayed on television. You should not even think of chasing a storm unless you have been properly trained. "Storm chasing," Reimer cautions, "is dangerous and has become sensationalized. If you're really interested in learning how to storm chase, start out by attending a free storm spotter training class provided by your local National Weather Service office."

One thing all storm chasers agree on is safety. Don't chase a storm unless you know what you are doing or are with someone who does. Caryn Hill's advice to the newcomer is to chase storms with those who have enough experience to keep you out of trouble. "There is a right way and a wrong way to chase," she says, "and if you aren't familiar enough with storms, you could quickly get yourself into trouble. Stay home or stay back if you are unsure of your abilities to safely chase. Getting too close isn't the answer to enjoying a storm!"

OTHER OPTIONS

NWS meteorologist Andrew Snyder points out that you don't have to be an official storm chaser to provide valuable information. One of the most important ways people can help the National Weather Service, he says, is to volunteer to submit weather information. This can be accomplished in several different ways and requires a minimal amount of training. Reports such as these are crucial during ongoing severe weather situations since these observers serve as the eyes in the field. Other than through information from sparsely spaced automated observing equipment, meteorologists have no way of knowing the exact conditions on the ground. The reports of eyewitnesses, especially during a crisis, can be critical. They allow for a better understanding of what is going on and can lead to better forecasts and warnings. In addition, many of these observations are stored as official weather data, giving a more complete climate record. This helps researchers and computer modelers in their work.

Another way to help is to be informed, Snyder says. "By understanding the weather, learning how to prepare, and knowing what safety precautions to take during hazardous situations, you can help keep yourself and others safe during dangerous weather."

CREATING YOUR OWN WEATHER STATION

The essential tools for a home weather station are a rain gauge, a wind gauge, a wind vane, a thermometer, a barometer, a hygrometer and a method for keeping records. Using simple materials, you can make everything yourself, except for the thermometer, which you can buy at a hardware store for just a few dollars.

To get the most out of these instruments, check them often and keep accurate records. You can use a simple paper notebook or make a folder on your computer to record your observations and to make graphs or charts. Try to check your weather instruments at least once every day, and write down the results of what you see. Doing this will allow you to see how the weather changes. You can also compare the weather of one month or season with another.

RAIN GAUGE

To make a rain gauge, which measures the amount of rain that falls during a storm, you'll need the following:
>   paper
>   scissors
>   glue (optional)
>   clear plastic tape
>   any straight-sided glass or plastic container
>   with a wide mouth
>   a rainy day

1. Cut a strip of paper smaller than the height of the container, and mark off in inches and fractions of inches (or in millimeters). Glue or tape the paper strip to the side of the container. Make sure that the numbers start at the bottom.

2. Cover the paper strip with the clear plastic tape so it will be waterproof.

3. Place your rain gauge outside. Make sure it's in a place that's not sheltered from the sky, such as under a tree or under the overhang of a roof. Measure the amount of rain that falls each time there is a storm.

WIND GAUGE

To make a wind gauge (also called an anemometer), which measures how fast the wind is blowing, you'll need the following:

glue
an empty thread spool
a piece of plywood 1 foot × 1 foot (0.3 m ×
     0.3 m)
scissors
a ruler
cardboard
a nail

a marking pen
thumbtacks
4 paper (or plastic) cups
a pencil with an eraser (use a brand-new
     pencil)
a stapler (optional)
a paper clip
a digital watch or a watch with a minute hand

1. Glue the spool to the center of the piece of plywood.

2. Cut two strips of cardboard measuring 2 inches × 18 inches (5 cm × 45.7 cm) each. Glue them together at the middle so they form an X.

3. Using the nail, punch a small hole in the exact center of the X. The hole should be larger than the pin on the thumbtack.

4. Make a mark on one of the cups with the marking pen. Then glue or staple a paper cup to the end of each arm of the X. Make sure they are all facing the same direction. That way when the wind hits the cups, the X will turn.

5. Straighten out at least half of the paper clip. Place the X onto the pencil so the hole in the X is over the eraser. Push the end of the straightened paper clip into the eraser. Place the other end of the pencil into the spool. Make sure the X is balanced and spins easily.

6. Using a watch, count the number of times the cup with the mark on it rotates in one minute. The number will be your wind speed in miles per hour. (To convert to kilometers per hour, multiply by 1.6.)

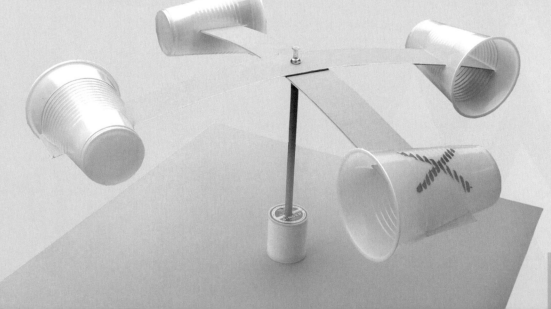

WIND VANE

A wind vane tells you from what direction the wind is coming. It is the simplest of all the instruments you can make, and you'll need the following:

a ruler
scissors
a piece of thin cardboard
a straw

tape
a paper clip
a pencil with an eraser (use a brand-new pencil)

1. Cut a square 3 inches (7.5 cm) on each side from the cardboard. Then cut out a triangle with 2-inch (5 cm) sides. The actual measurements aren't too important, but the square must be larger than the triangle.

2. Place one end of the straw onto the square. The end of the straw should be at about the middle of the square. Tape it in place. Do the same to the other end with the triangle so the two pieces of cardboard form an arrow.

3. Straighten out part of the paper clip, and push it through the center of the straw into the pencil eraser. Make sure that the straw is balanced.

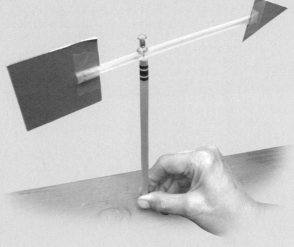

When you take your wind vane outdoors, the arrow will point in the direction the wind is coming from. Using a compass, you will be able to tell whether this is north, south, east, or west.

In the Northern Hemisphere, if the wind is coming from the
> north: expect cold weather;
> south: expect warm weather;
> east: there may be precipitation (rain or snow);
> west: the weather will be clearing.

In the Southern Hemisphere, if the wind is coming from the
> north: expect warm weather;
> south: expect cold weather;
> east: the weather will be clearing;
> west: there may be precipitation (rain or snow).

BAROMETER

A barometer measures differences in air pressure from day to day. A significant change in air pressure usually means a change in the weather. Be sure to place your barometer somewhere that doesn't experience many temperature changes. Keep it away from windows, for instance. Changes in temperature will cause the air inside the bottle to expand or contract. This will give you false readings.

To make your own barometer, you'll need the following:

a plastic soda bottle
food coloring
a clear plastic drinking straw
a cork or rubber stopper with a hold in the
    middle or a glob of clay or putty (if
    the cork or stopper doesn't already
    have a hole through it, have an adult
    bore one for you)
a marking pen

1. Fill the bottle a little over halfway with water. Add a few drops of food coloring (any color you like!).

2. Insert the straw into the stopper, and then place the stopper in the neck of the bottle. If you don't have a stopper, you can use some clay or putty to seal the opening. Make sure that the end of the straw is below the surface of the water.

3. Blow into the straw until you've made a few bubbles. When you stop blowing, the water will rise up into the straw.

4. Use the marker to mark the point on the straw where the water level is.

5. Changes in atmospheric pressure will cause the level of water in the tube to rise or fall. Increased air pressure will make the liquid fall. Decreased pressure will cause it to rise. Check your barometer several times each day, and keep a record of whether the air pressure has risen or fallen. Changes in air pressure often indicate changes in the weather. High pressure is usually associated with nice weather, while low air pressure is often a sign of storms.

HYGROMETER

Humidity is an indication of how much moisture is in the air. A hygrometer measures this humidity. This is an important thing to know because the more moisture there is in the air, the more likely it will rain or snow (depending on the temperature). To make your own hygrometer, you will need the following:

an empty 1-quart (1-liter) milk carton
scissors
a large sewing needle
a file card or a piece of stiff paper
glue
a paper clip

an oil-free, freshly shampooed human hair at least 9 inches (23 cm) long
tape (optional)
a penny or other small coin
a wet towel

1. Clean the carton so there is no milk in it. Place the carton on its side.

2. Near the bottom, cut an H-shaped slit. Pull up the two tabs, and bend them so they are upright. Push the needle through the tabs.

3. Cut a slender piece of file card or stiff paper. This will be your indicator. You can copy the one on page 55 at 125 percent. Push one end of the needle through the end of the indicator, and hold it in place with a drop of glue.

4. At the other end of the milk carton, cut a small slit and insert the paper clip so only a small loop shows.

5. Tie one end of the hair to the paper clip, wind it two or three times around the needle, and then tape or glue the penny to the other end. Lay the carton on its side, and let the penny dangle over the end of the milk carton as shown.

6. Copy the scale on page 55 onto the card (can be copied at 125 percent). Tape or glue it onto the side of the carton right below the end of the needle.

7. Place the finished hygrometer onto a wet towel. Set the indicator so it is vertical. Wait 15 minutes and see which way the indicator has moved. Mark the line nearest to the end of the indicator as "10." This will be the highest measurement of humidity.

8. Take the hygrometer off the towel, and place it somewhere where it won't be disturbed and where there won't be any sudden changes in humidity such as a bedroom or a porch. As the hair dries, it will begin to shrink. This will rotate the needle, causing the indicator to move toward the lower numbers—the dry end—of the scale. Humid air makes the hair stretch, and dry air makes it shrink. As the humidity in the air increases or decreases, the indicator will move accordingly.

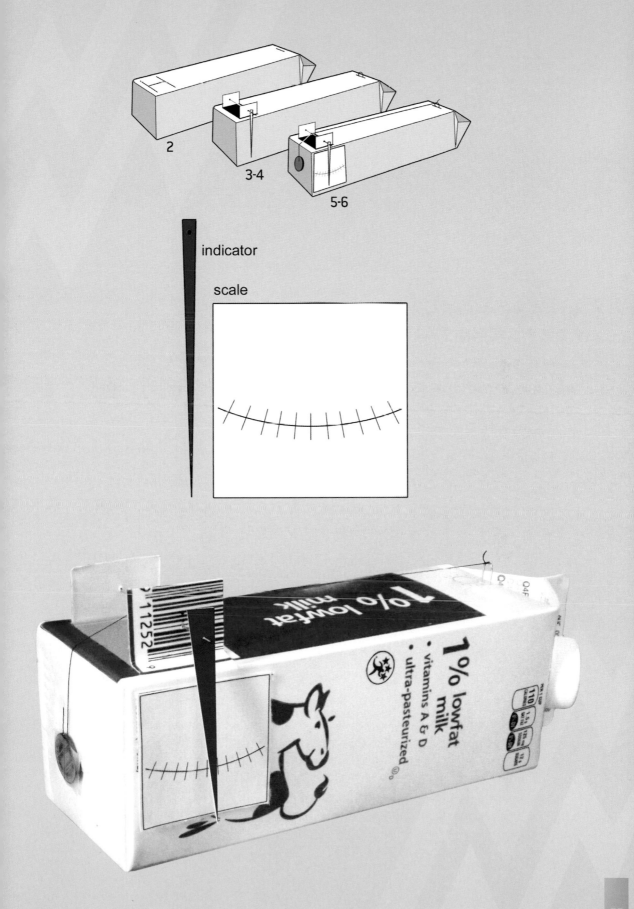

2

3-4

5-6

indicator

scale

WEATHER EMERGENCY KIT

It is a good idea to have an emergency weather kit on hand for severe weather emergencies. In extreme conditions, a storm can leave you without power, food, water, communication devices, and shelter. The kit should contain the following:

- 1 gallon (4 liters) of water per person per day for at least three days, for drinking and sanitation

- At least a three-day supply of nonperishable food

- A sleeping bag or a warm blanket for each person

- A complete change of clothing, including a long-sleeved shirt, long pants, and sturdy shoes

- A fire extinguisher and matches in a waterproof container

- Personal hygiene items, paper cups, plates, plastic utensils, and paper towels

- A battery-powered or hand-crank radio and a NOAA weather radio with tone alert and extra batteries for both. (Weather radios are inexpensive radios permanently tuned to the NOAA Weather Radio network. It broadcasts warnings, watches, forecasts, and other hazard information twenty-four hours a day, seven days a week.)

- A flashlight and extra batteries

- A first aid kit

- A whistle to signal for help

- Dust masks (to help filter contaminated air) and plastic sheeting and duct tape for making a shelter

- Moist towelettes, garbage bags, and plastic ties for personal sanitation

- A wrench or a pliers to turn off utilities

- A can opener for food (if kit contains canned food)

- Local maps

Additional personal items should include prescription medications and spare glasses, infant formula and diapers, pet food and extra water for your pets, and some cash. Protect important family documents, such as copies of insurance policies, identification, bank account records, and meaningful family photos in a waterproof, portable container. This would include any computer disks or flash drives containing important information.

Paper and pencils, books, games, puzzles, and other games can help pass the time. Other ideas and suggestions for weather emergency preparation are available from the Federal Emergency Management Agency at http://www.fema.gov.

SOURCE NOTES

6 George Kourounis, interview with the author, March 15, 2013.

6 Roger Hill, interview with the author, March 15, 2013.

6 David Reimer, interview with the author, March15, 2013.

6 Ibid.

7 Caryn Hill, interview with the author, May 8, 2013.

8 Roger Hill, interview.

8 Kourounis, interview.

8–9 Ibid.

9 Jack Williams, *The Weather Book* (New York: Vintage Books, 1997), 120.

10 Kourounis, interview.

12 Ibid.

20 Roger Hill, interview.

30 Steve Rudin, interview with the author, February 14, 2013.

32 Andrew Snyder, interview with the author, January 10, 2013.

33 Ibid.

34 Ibid.

41–42 Kourounis, interview.

44 Rudin, interview.

44 Roger Hill, interview.

44 Reimer, interview.

45 Ibid.

45 Ibid.

45–46 Kourounis, interview.

46 Caryn Hill, interview.

47 Kourounis, interview.

47 Roger Hill, interview.

47–48 Reimer, interview.

48 Caryn Hill, interview.

48 Reimer, interview.

48 Caryn Hill, interview.

49 Snyder, interview.

atmosphere: the layer of gas that surrounds Earth

climate: the general or average weather conditions of a certain region, including temperature, rainfall, and wind

Coriolis effect: an effect of Earth's rotation that causes wind to move in circular patterns

cyclone: any storm that moves in a circular direction

Doppler radar: a system that measures the speed and direction of a storm

global warming: a gradual increase in Earth's average temperature

greenhouse effect: a warming effect created by gases in the atmosphere trapping heat from the sun

humidity: the measure of the amount of water in the atmosphere

hurricane: a strong, rotating tropical storm

mesocyclone: a rapidly rotating mass of air inside a thunderstorm that often gives rise to tornadoes

mesosphere: the region of Earth's atmosphere lying above the stratosphere and below the thermosphere. The mesosphere lies between about 31 and 50 miles (50 to 80 km) above Earth's surface.

meteorologist: a scientist who studies weather and climate

meteorology: the science of weather and climate

stratosphere: the region of Earth's atmosphere extending from the top of the troposphere to about 31 miles (50 km) above Earth's surface

supercell: a thunderstorm with a powerful, rotating updraft

thermosphere: the region of Earth's upper atmosphere lying between a height of approximately 50 miles (80 km) to between 341 and 434 miles (550 and 700 km) above Earth's surface

tornado: a rapidly rotating column of air

troposphere: the lowest layer of Earth's atmosphere. It is the layer in which most weather takes place. It extends to about 10 miles (16 km) above the surface of Earth.

weather: the condition of the atmosphere at any particular time and place

wind shear: a sudden change in wind direction and speed between different altitudes

SELECTED BIBLIOGRAPHY

Ahrens, C. Donald. *Meteorology Today*. Belmont, CA: Brooks Cole, 2013.

Burt, Stephen. *The Weather Observer's Handbook*. Cambridge: Cambridge University Press, 2012.

Flannery, Tim. *The Weather Makers*. New York: Grove Press, 2001.

Forrester, Frank H. *1001 Questions Answered about the Weather*. New York: Dover Publications, 1981.

Fry, Julian. *The Encyclopedia of Weather and Climate Change*. Berkeley: University of California Press, 2010.

Ludlin, F. H., and R. S. Scorer. *Cloud Study*. London: John Murray, 1957.

Murchie, Guy. *Song of the Sky*. Boston: Houghton Mifflin, 1954.

Sandlin, Lee. *Storm Kings*. New York: Pantheon, 2013.

Scientific American. *Storm Warning*s. New York: Scientific American, 2012.

Scorer, Richard. *Clouds of the World*. Harrisburg, PA: Stackpole Books, 1972.

Williams, Jack. *The Weather Book*. New York: Vintage Books, 1997.

LERNER
SOURCE

Expand learning beyond the printed book. Download free, complementary educational resources for this book from our website, www.lerneresource.com.

BOOKS

Breen, Mark. *Kids' Book of Weather Forecasting.* Danbury, CT: Ideals, 2008.

Cosgrove, Brian. *Weather*. London: Dorling Kindersley, 2007.

Fleisher, Paul. *Lightning, Hurricanes, and Blizzards: The Science of Storms*. Minneapolis: Lerner Publications Company, 2010.

Fradin, Judy. *Tornado! The Story behind These Twisting, Turning, Spinning, and Spiraling Storms*. Washington, DC: National Geographic Children's Books, 2011.

Furgang, Kathy. *Everything Weather*. Washington, DC: National Geographic Children's Books, 2012.

Gaffney, Timothy R. *Storm Scientist: Careers Chasing Severe Weather.* Wild Science Careers series. Berkeley Heights, NJ: Enslow Publishers, 2009.

Hill, Roger, and Peter Bronski. *Hunting Nature's Fury*. Berkeley, CA: Wilderness Press, 2009.

Hollingshead, Mike. *Adventures in Tornado Alley: The Storm Chasers*. London: Thames & Hudson, 2008.

Mogil, H. Michael. *Extreme Weather.* New York: Simon & Schuster, 2011.

Reed, Jim. *Storm Chaser: A Photographer's Journey*. New York: Abrams, 2009.

Sandlin, Lee. *Storm Kings: The Untold History of America's First Tornado Chasers*. New York: Pantheon, 2013.

Simon, Seymour. *Hurricanes*. New York: HarperCollins, 2007.

Snedecker, Joe. *The Everything KIDS' Weather Book: From Tornadoes to Snowstorms, Puzzles, Games, and Facts That Make Weather for Kids Fun!* Cincinnati: Adams Media, 2012.

Vasquez, Tim. *Storm Chasing Handbook*. Garland, TX: Weather Graphics, 2009.

Yeager, Paul. *Weather Whys: Facts, Myths, and Oddities*. New York: Perigee Book, 2010.

WEBSITES

George Kourounis
http://www.stormchaser.ca
The official website of storm chaser George Kourounis has amazing photos and video footage of storms, as well as links to his appearances on radio and television and information about his storm-chasing equipment.

Home Weather Station
http://www.salemclock.com/weather/weather01.htm
This site offers everything you need to know to build and operate your own home weather station.

Hurricane Hunters, NOAA
http://flightscience.noaa.gov/
This is the official website of NOAA's hurricane hunters. The site has a photo gallery of different types of storms, and you can learn more about what the hunters do and how they do it.

Hurricane Hunters, US Navy
http://www.navyhurricanehunters.com/
This is the official website of the US Navy's Hurricane Hunters. You can learn more about the history of the navy's Hurricane Hunters, watch a slide show, and get a quick overview of Hurricane Hunter flight facts.

National Weather Service
http://www.weather.gov/
The official website of the National Weather Service offers forecasting information, great imagery, maps, historical weather data, kids activities, safety tips, and more.

NWS Cooperative Observer Program
http://www.nws.noaa.gov/om/coop/index.htm
Check out this website to learn how to join the National Weather Service Cooperative Observer Program and become a weather spotter.

Skywarn
http://www.nws.noaa.gov/skywarn/
This website provides information about the Skywarn weather-spotting program and how to become a volunteer member.

Storm Chasing Tours
http://www.cloud9tours.com/
http://www.tempesttours.com/
Both of these services offer tours led by professional storm chasers. This is the safest way to see a tornado. The tours are expensive, but the sites have some cool photos and videos of storms.

Storm Prediction Center

http://www.spc.noaa.gov/

This website has a wide range of forecasting tools, maps and other weather data, safety tips, storm reports, and more.

The Texas Storm Chasers

http://www.texasstormchasers.com/

The official website of the Texas Storm Chasers, a group of amateur storm chasers from all over the state, has maps and other weather data along with a great library of storm videos.

Tornadoscapes

http://www.stormchase.net/

The official website of professional storm chasers Roger and Caryn Hill offers video footage of storms along with written accounts of storm-chasing trips in various part of the United States.

Weather Wiz Kids

http://www.weatherwizkids.com/

This is an excellent website for kids of all ages (adults too), created by professional meteorologist Crystal Wicker. The site has all kinds of great information about weather, with quizzes, activities, photos, games, and even a section devoted to weather jokes. You can also learn how to pursue a career in weather and send questions to Crystal on the Ask Crystal page.

INDEX

ABOUT THE AUTHOR

Hugo Award-winning author and illustrator Ron Miller specializes in books about science. *Curiosity's Mission on Mars: Exploring the Red Planet, Is the End of the World Near? From Crackpot Predictions to Scientific Scenarios,* and *Recentering the Universe: The Radical Theories of Copernicus, Kepler, Galileo, and Newton* are among his recent titles. His favorite subjects are space and astronomy. A postage stamp he created is currently on board a spaceship headed for Pluto. His original paintings can be found in collections all over the world. Miller lives in Virginia.

PHOTO ACKNOWLEDGMENTS

The images in this book are used with the permission of: Courtesy of the NOAA Photo Library, pp. 1, 14, 33, 38; © iStockphoto.com/ninjaMonkeyStudio, pp. 4, 15, 25 (top), 32, 39, 44; © Andra Cerar/Dreamstime.com, pp. 4–5 (background); © Carlo Allegri/Getty Images, p. 5 (inset); © Ron Miller, pp. 7, 16, 18, 19, 20, 21, 24, 27, 50, 51, 52, 53, 55 (top and bottom); © Ryan K. McGinnis/Alamy, pp. 8, 47; © MANDEL NGAN/AFP/Getty Images, p. 9; © Jim Reed/CORBIS, p. 10; © Gregg Williams/Dreamstime.com, pp. 11, 13, 41; © Jim Reed/RGB Ventures LLC/Alamy, p. 12; © Cavan Images/Getty Images, p. 23; © Justin Sullivan/Getty Images, p. 25 (bottom); © iStockphoto.com/ssuaphoto, p. 29; AP Photo/Charlie Riedel, p. 30; © Caryn Hill, p. 35; AP Photo/Alan Diaz, p. 36; AP Photo/David Goldman, p. 42; © Jim Edds/ CORBIS, p. 43; © Mike Hollingshead/Science Faction/Corbis, p. 46; © Ted Russell/Time & Life Pictures/Getty Images, p. 48.

Front Cover: © Jim Reed/Science Faction/SuperStock.
Back Cover: Courtesy of the NOAA Photo Library.

Main body text set in Conduit ITC Std Medium 12.5/21.
Typeface provided by International Typeface Corp.